I love you so

Written by Jill Kingwell

Illustrated by Kelly Cazzaniga

AuthorHouse™
1663 Liberty Drive
Bloomington, IN 47403
www.authorhouse.com
Phone: 833-262-8899

This book is printed on acid-free paper.

ISBN: 978-1-4389-5126-3 (sc)

Print information available on the last page.

Published by AuthorHouse 02/21/2025

authorHOUSE®

Dedicated to William Kingwell

Our story "I love you so" is a story we hope will be told to sick children, healthy children, children with sick loved ones around the world. Our first story is told with charming illustrations and a simple yet cherished poem about a child and his sick grandpa. I love you so, I want you here to see me grow is a special book that touches one's heart and is cherished for the importance of love, loss and lasting memories. We hope this new series of books "I love you so" will be successful and proceeds will be donated to a children's hospital to help with research and finding a cure for cancer.

You are my favorite,
I love you so

I want you here
to see me grow

I've had my Grandpa
for only a few short years

To which I have grown
so near and dear

Today I found out that Grandpa is sick

and treatment will help
but may not fix

Grandpa will get weak before he gets better

needing my love
now more than ever

I will be by your side every step of the way

Knowing you will get better
day-by-day

Now it is my turn to be by your side when you are weak

Knowing you will get better
week-by-week

You are my favorite, I Love You So

I want you here to see me grow

I Love You Grandpa

The End

About the Author

   I am now in my 30's with a Business Marketing degree and a passion for writing. With the help of one of my cherished friends my illustrator and her creativity we have decided that our story is to help parents, grandparents, caregivers, and respected adults tell the hardest story of all, one that involves love and loss. We both have small children and sick loved ones and a passion to tell our story in a book with warm and touching illustrations. Our hope is that our series of "I love you so" will continue to help children understand the importance of love, loss, relationships and most importantly making lasting memories.

Printed in the United States
by Baker & Taylor Publisher Services